‘The field … o labour’

Watercolours by Robert Hills (1769-1844) and his contemporaries

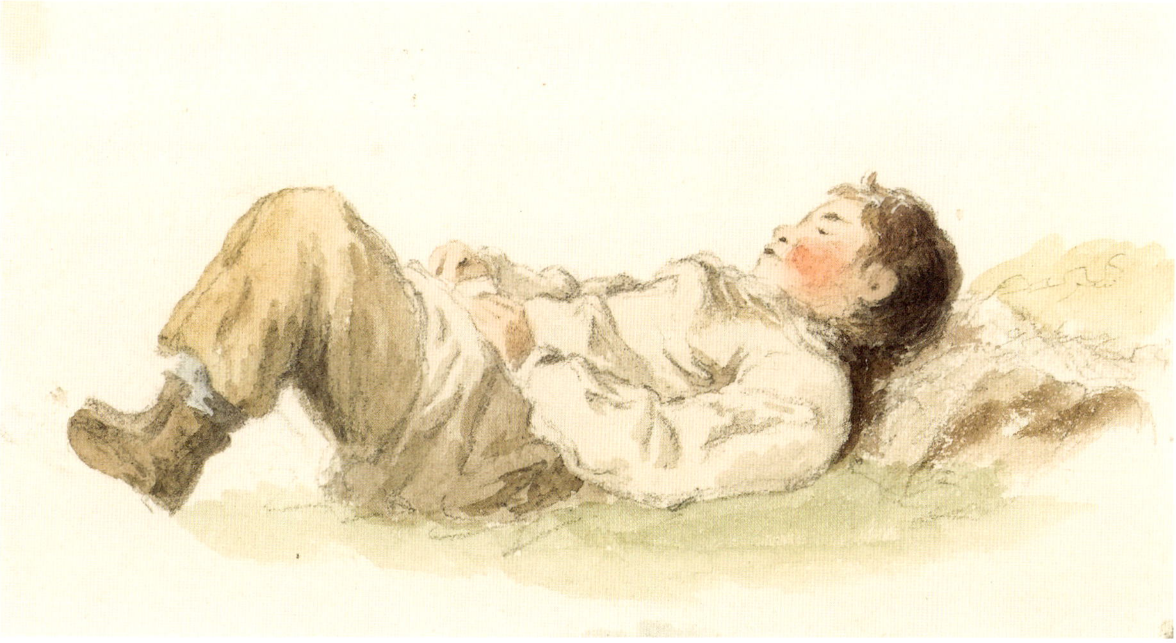

Robert Hills is not a name familiar to most museum visitors in the twenty-first century, but he was at the vanguard of watercolour painting in Britain at the turn of the nineteenth century. This alone would merit a timely re-examination of his work in relation to better known contemporaries such as David Cox and Peter De Wint but his evident sensitivity toward the landscape, and its inhabitants, also strikes a chord today, appealing to both our interest in rural history and our concerns about the future of the countryside.

Robert Hills was born on June 26th 1769, in Islington, London. He took drawing lessons from John Alexander Gresse (1741-94), who excelled at watercolours of landscapes. Hills first exhibited at the Royal Academy in 1791, having enrolled as a student there three years previously. Along with William Henry Pyne (1769-1843) and James Ward (1769-1859), Hills was part of the Sketching Society, which met regularly from 1800 at the house of each member in turn, sometimes welcoming thirty or forty other artists as guests.[1] On November 30th 1804, Hills became one the founding members of the Society of Painters in Watercolours (SPW), along with William Wells, Samuel Shelley, W. H. Pyne, Nicholas Pocock, John and Cornelius Varley, John Claude Nattes and William Sawrey Gilpin. Membership was limited to twenty-four, who were to have been of ‘moral character’, ‘professional reputation’ and ‘resident in the United Kingdom’.[2] The Society's first exhibition was held the following April. Their aim was to achieve what the Royal Academy had for its members in 1768; public recognition, a place to show and sell their work, and, as they all taught, a place where students could learn more about the technique and practice of watercolour. Furthermore, watercolours tended to be badly hung at the Academy, usually situated, as Hills noted, ‘between windows and under windows, sometimes in the darkened room with the sculpture, where if they had merit, it could not be seen’.[3] The first exhibition was a rousing success; during the six-week run, 12,000 people paid an admission fee of 1/-.[4]

As a result of the SPW's restrictions on the number of exhibitors, a rival society was set up; members of the New Society of Painters in Miniature and Water-Colours, or the Associated Artists, as they became know, included David Cox (1783-1859) and Peter De Wint (1784-1849). However, what began as fair rivalry turned to disaster – their exhibitions were too similar, and the preponderance of landscape painting meant they inevitably competed for similar ground.[5] On its eighth anniversary the SPW was dissolved; a new Society of Painters in Oil and Water-Colour, embracing the two media, was then formed. This decision was reversed in 1820, however, when those in favour of watercolour's independence re-grouped as the ‘Old Water-Colour Society’.[6] Hills was re-elected a member in 1823; in 1827 he was elected Treasurer, and was appointed Secretary in 1831, retaining that position until his death in 1844.[7] Not much is known about Hills's personal life. He was not married but evidently had a wide circle of friends and acquaintances, indeed, he was so highly thought of by his fellow Society members that they presented him with a plate to the value of 100 guineas in 1809 to celebrate his unremitting service to the Society since its establishment.

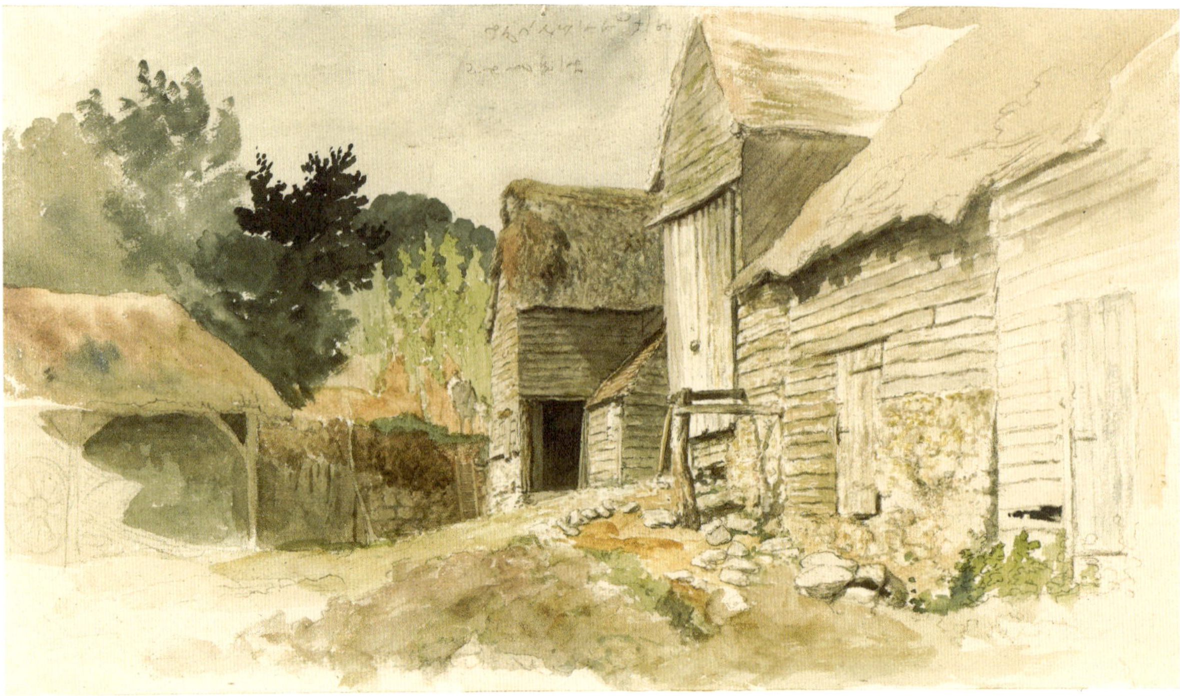

30. Robert Hills, *Study of barns*

The development of watercolour painting

The vogue for watercolour painting peaked in the first decade of the nineteenth century and was linked indissolubly with topographical view painting, where careful observation and exact rendering formed the basis for antiquarian and geographical study. New techniques were being employed and, in response, new types of papers and an increasing number of pigments entered the market, making watercolour appear more modern and forward-looking than oil. Cheaper and quicker than oil, the work of watercolour artists also better suited the modest pretensions of a modern patron, restricted by domestic space and budget.

Watercolour was most effectively and creatively employed where transparency and a reflected brilliance from the white ground of the paper was exploited. The paper surface was never entirely smooth; variations in texture reflected different amounts of light even when layers of wash were passed over them. The alternation of light and shadow was considered especially advantageous for representing distances in landscape, and gave a subtlety to aerial tints that oil could not provide.[8] Under the impetus of various technological developments within the growing English paper industry, several makers began to produce very particular papers to satisfy highly specific demands, which allowed painters to explore the luminosity of the white ground by leaving the paper to sparkle as highlights through loose washes of colour (see nos. 37 and 39). Colourmen such as Newman, Reeve, Rowney, and Winsor and Newton relieved the artist of the tedium of mixing his own colours with advances in ready-to-use pigments,[9] such as Emerald Green and French Ultramarine, which came on the market in the 1820s.[10]

Rural Britain at the turn of the nineteenth century

The emergence of rustic landscape painting as a major genre in England at the end of the eighteenth century coincided with the accelerated enclosure of the English countryside.[11] During the reign of George III over 3,500 Enclosure Acts had enclosed 5 million acres of land with devastating effect on the communal England that had existed up to that point.[12] The countryside was reorganised to appropriate much of England by restructuring the land into what essentially became small, privately owned fields.

The ongoing Napoleonic wars also impacted upon the rural landscape. Large wartime profits increased rents and taxation, the burden of which was almost wholly carried by the farming community. Even after the end of the wars in 1815, taxation remained high, while agricultural profits and the value of land dramatically declined. Large numbers of landowners and farmers went bankrupt and the majority of agricultural labourers were left jobless. The result was a steady depopulation of rural areas.[13] During the late eighteenth century farmers in the south and east had turned from dairy to wheat production – another result of the war which drove up the demand and cost of wheat while giving farmers a protected market.[14] However, crop failures and a bad harvest in 1794-95 resulted in food riots, and these continued into nineteenth century.[15] Moreover, the increase in population from 6 million to 9 million in the latter half of the eighteenth century resulted in a population which outstripped work opportunities, the consequences of which were most famously discussed in the Rev. Malthus's (1766-1834) controversial publication, *Essay on the Principle of Population* (1798), in which he argued that the population was kept in balance with the food supply by a series of checks, including war and famine.

The effect of the countryside upon painters and poets

The title of this exhibition, 'the field calls me to labour', is taken from an eighteenth-century poem, *To a Gentleman*, the first recorded verse written by the 'thresher poet', Stephen Duck (1705-56), best-known for his poem, *The Thresher's Labour* (1730). As a consequence of the economic and social situation, there was a growing awareness in the first half of the nineteenth century that a particular physical and social environment, and its way of life, was disappearing at the hands of agricultural and social change.[16] While the old open field system was inefficient, and the population increase and demand for agricultural produce towards the end of the eighteenth century led to an expanding market, there was still nostalgia for the old system; in *The Shepherd's Calendar* of 1827, the poet John Clare (1793-1864) wrote, 'Enclosure came, and trampled on the grave / Of labour's rights and left the poor a slave'.[17] In artistic terms, between 1780 and 1815 there was a shift away from idealised pastoral landscape painting to an increasing interest in naturalistic landscapes and portrayals of real-life labourers; at the same time, the war with France prevented artists from travelling freely across Europe, and they turned instead to the English countryside for inspiration. Increasingly sentimental genre scenes and escapist idylls of contemporary rural life began to appear in watercolourists' work, reflecting a prevailing disenchantment with visible changes in the countryside and the need for reassurance in a time of threats of revolution.[18]

The majority of examples of Hills's work in this exhibition are multiple studies, painted on the same sheet, and are highly typical of his style, in the precise attention to textures of clothing and the fur of animals,

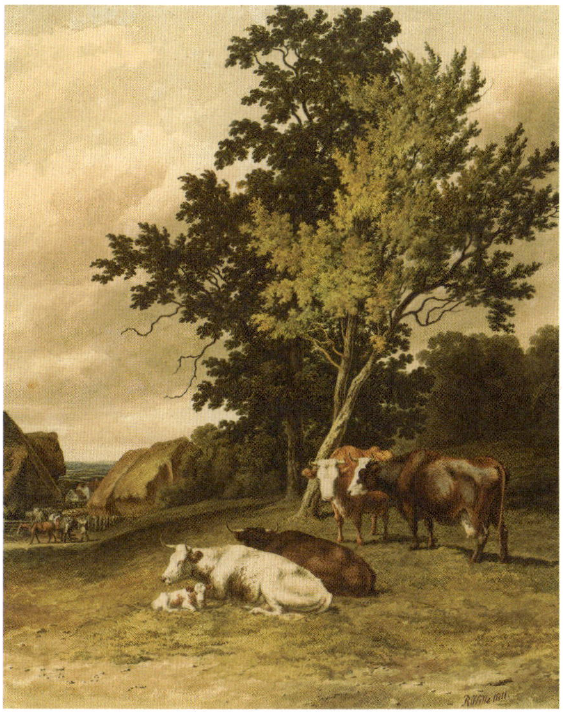

27. Robert Hills, *Landscape with cattle, near Dorking, Surrey*

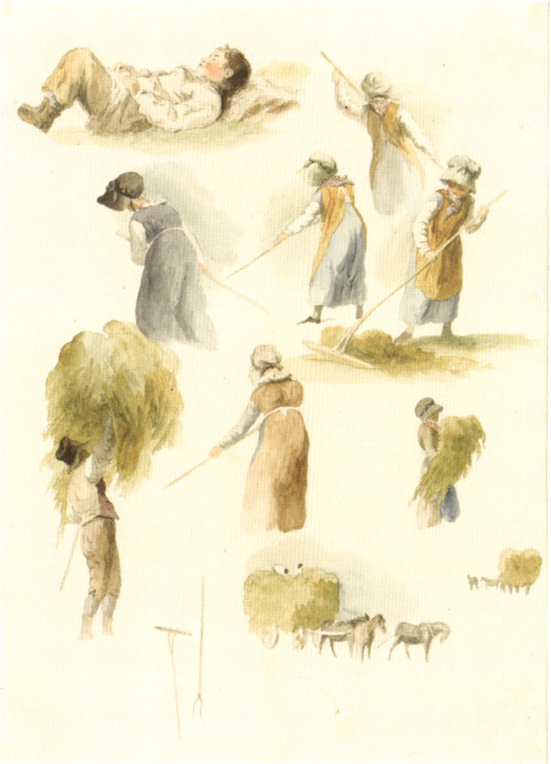

36. Robert Hills, *Studies of children haymaking*

clarity of atmosphere, sense of space, and fresh, clean colour. In *Rudiments of Landscape Drawing*, W. H. Pyne wrote of Hills that 'every image is strictly rural – the labourers are engaged in appropriate employments . . . his horses are not only of the cart breed, but of that peculiar character identified in the farmer's team; his cows are not of a uniform size or colour, but appear to have been purchased at various times and at different fairs' (see nos. 10, 11, 22, 40).[19] He frequently painted at Windsor Park and the Lake District, but also in Surrey. In later life he turned his attention to Kent and picturesque farmyards. His sketches are frequently annotated in shorthand, though not apparently in any of the usual methods: a code still to be cracked, his, and James Ward's, use of shorthand has baffled generations of art historians (no. 26).[20]

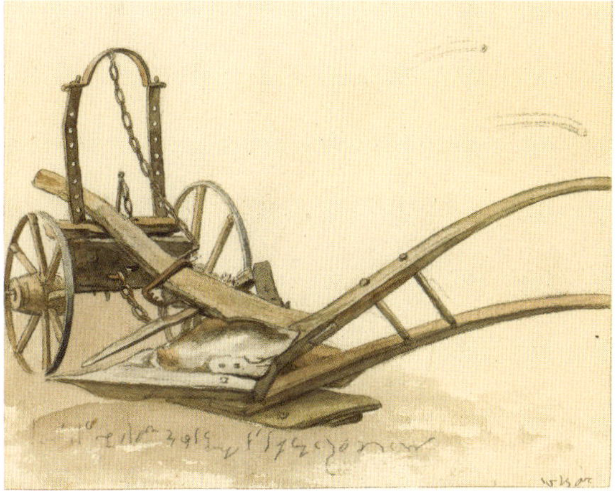

32. Robert Hills, *Study of ploughs*

While Hills's sketches consist of washes of colour, his later work intended for more public display employed bodycolour, which added depth and texture to a watercolour painting, and helped it compete with oil painting, specifically on gallery walls, where the intensity of colour was attractive to potential buyers. Moreover, he put the technique of stippling to new use by employing a loose system to flecks and dots that gave his work a textural density approximating that of oil (no. 27).[21] While Hills's treatment of figures, tools, and animals is somewhat reminiscent of Ward's close attention to such subjects, it differs dramatically from that of Cox and De Wint, whose often grandiose rural landscapes are generally left unpeopled (De Wint's *Harvesters Resting*, no. 41, is an atypical example).

While developments in the countryside left many concerned for its future, such progress was also viewed as economically advantageous. To an uncritical eye the British countryside would have shown much to admire, and the artists would have shared this admiration.[22] In this exhibition, people are shown working the land, or at rest, after a hard day's work. These images of farm labourers offer a positive representation which did not directly echo real life, though Pyne, in *Etchings of Rustic Figures for the Embellishment of Landscape* (1814), advocated studying people from life, on the spot, so that the groups will 'assume the air of nature'.[23] Rosy-cheeked youngsters are shown in spotless clothing, not rags, and with bountiful harvests (nos. 36 & 42), hardly conforming to William Cobbett's stark image of the countryside, and his appeal in the 1820s for people to 'go into the villages and look at the miserable sheds in which the labourers reside . . . survey the rags on the backs of the wretched inhabitants'.[24]

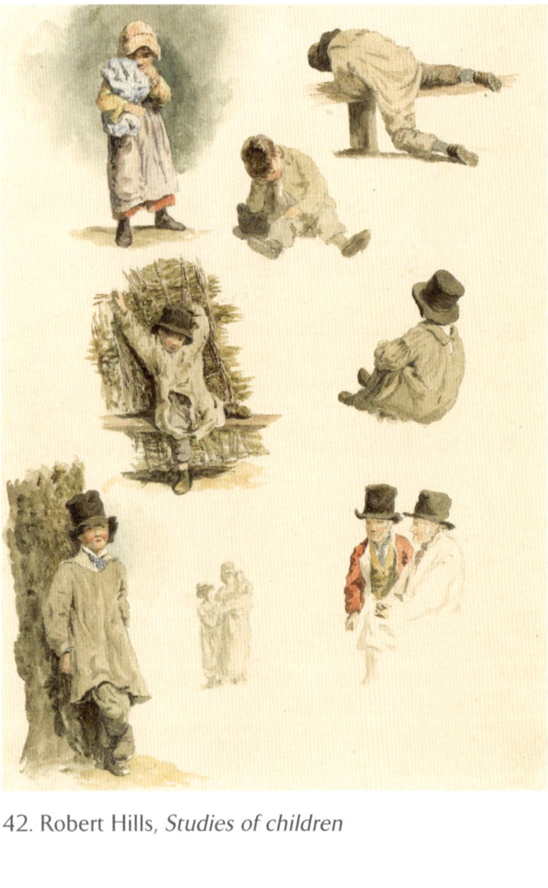

42. Robert Hills, *Studies of children*

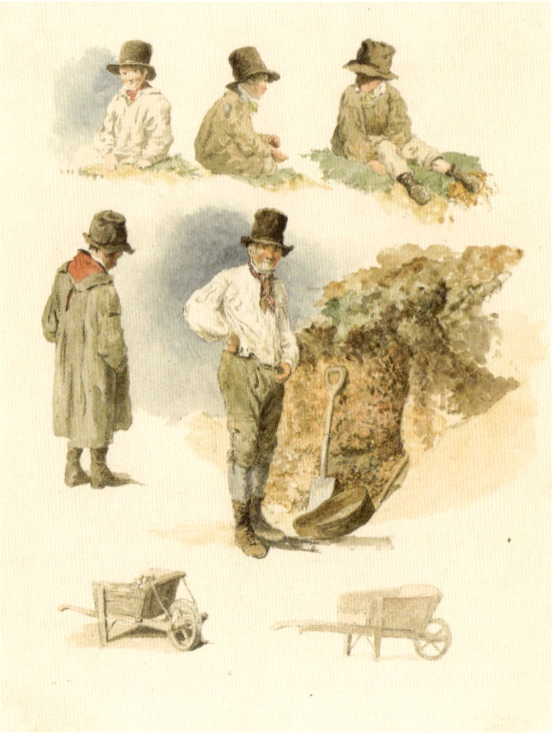

40. Robert Hills, *Studies of a gardener, children and wheelbarrows*

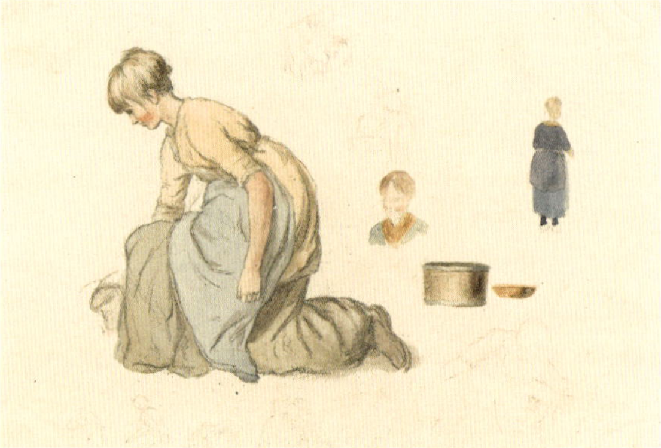

35. Robert Hills, *Studies of a ? milkmaid*

Pyne also discussed agricultural machinery, and it is clear that he and Hills shared an opinion of how machinery should be treated; 'a pump or well, a wheelbarrow, a cart, plough, or other object, if not represented with attention to mechanical construction, instead of adding to the interest of the piece, really deteriorates its merit' (nos. 31-33).[25] The early nineteenth century was the beginning of a period of technological advances, and this had clear implications for farm labourers.[26] But while the demand for threshers was high during the labour-source years of the Napoleonic wars, it fell sharply thereafter.[27]

Animal studies formed a large part of Hills's oeuvre; between 1795 and 1815, he produced 780 etchings of various animals, intended, like Pyne's *Rustic Figures*, for artists who wanted characteristic poses or groups of animals with which to embellish their landscapes (nos. 19, 22). Many watercolour artists, including Hills

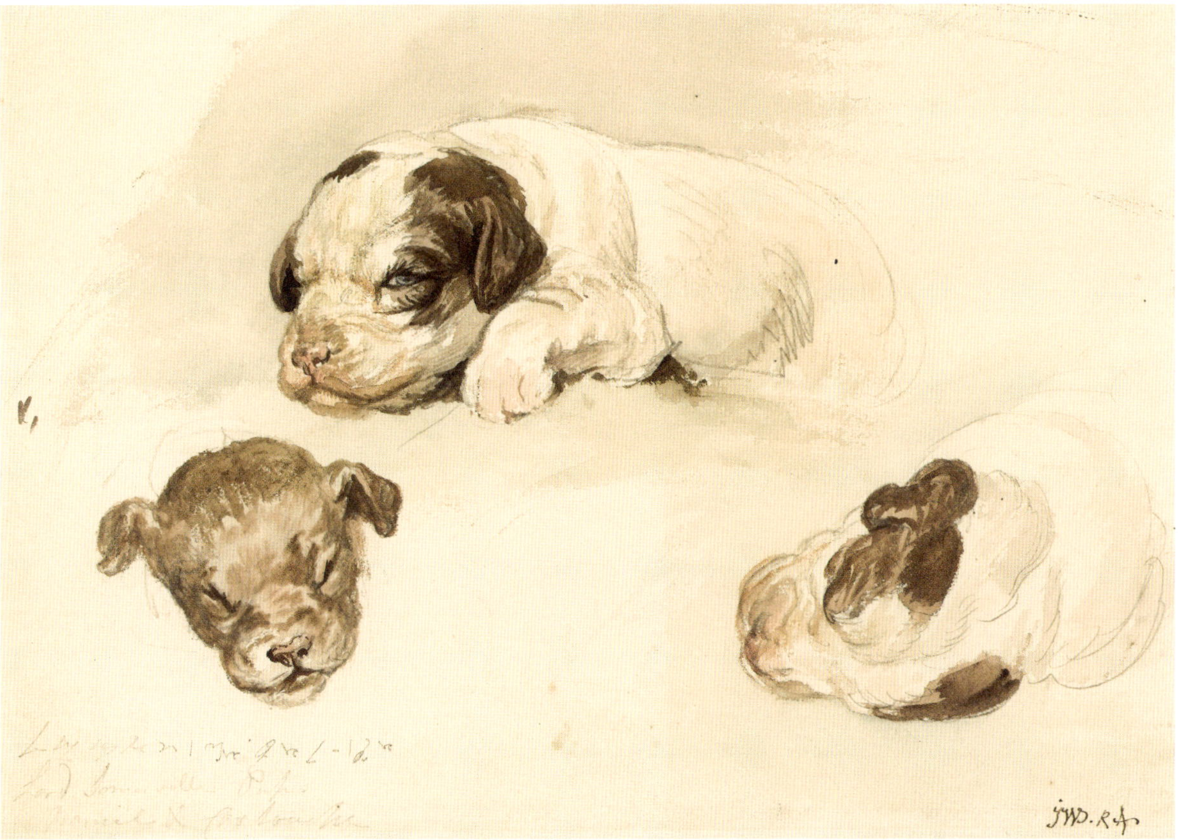

7. James Ward, *Study of Lord Somerville's puppies*

and Pyne, supported their income through teaching, and the turn of the nineteenth century saw a revolution in drawing manuals. Pyne described Robert Hills's *Etchings of Animals drawn from nature* as 'the most celebrated work designed for this purpose, and should be possessed by all who feel desirous of acquiring a just knowledge of their picturesque character', as they 'comprise all that is excellent in the study of domestic animals'.[28]

It was also within the realm of animal painting that James Ward is perhaps best known. At the turn of the nineteenth century, Ward received a major commission, most likely from Lord John Somerville (1765-1819), to produce a series of portraits examining the pedigree of livestock in Britain for the recently-established Board of Agriculture (nos. 12 & 14). The Board had initiated a number of pioneering surveys of the state of British agriculture and their intention was to promote knowledge of farming conditions throughout the country.[29] Just as rustic landscapes were seen to promote a harmonious and bountiful English countryside, this commission clearly had nationalistic overtones in the face of potential invasion from France. Though the project was never completed, it provided Ward with useful clients within the circle of landed gentry and estate owners.

Of the immediately succeeding generation of artists to focus on animal subjects, the most outstanding were John Frederick Lewis (1805-76; nos. 3 and 6) and Edwin Landseer (1802-73; nos. 1 and 2). For animal painters from the late 1820s onwards, the Zoological Gardens, which opened in Regent's Park in 1828, offered more exciting and dramatic examples of animal life. In 1839, Hills was asked to paint the first giraffe to be born at the Zoo.[30] William Harvey (1796-1866), a pupil of the wood-engraver Thomas Bewick, produced a series of drawings of zoo inhabitants (no. 23), and provided illustrations for *The Tower Menagerie* (1829), written by the zoologist Edward Turner Bennett (1797-1836). Edward Julius Detmold's (1883-1957) watercolour, *The Chimpanzee* (no. 24), perfectly captures the late nineteenth-century fascination with non-native species which gathered pace particularly after publication of Charles Darwin's *On the Origin of Species* (1859). Indeed, Detmold and his brother grew up near the Gardens and spent their childhoods making sketches of various inhabitants of the Zoo.

As one of the leading exponents of watercolour painting, Robert Hills's work is both innovative in technique and original in his treatment of rural topicality. He was clearly fascinated by the people who lived off the land, in their costumes and attitudes, and in the tools and animals they used in their daily life. In many ways, Hills, and his contemporaries, also present parallels with issues that affect rural regions today. Uncertainties continue to face the countryside as issues such as climate change and rising food prices affect our fields, while articles on global hunger and self-sufficiency appear in the media on an almost daily basis.[31] The countryside was revered by watercolour artists at the turn of the nineteenth century who offered a view of a more honest and potentially harmonious life. Hills may not always convey to viewers the harsher side of rural life, but he does show a sensitive respect for the hard, physical work of the labourer and the farm animal.

Checklist of Exhibits

Exhibits are ordered according to the display at the Fitzwilliam Museum, 27 May - 7 September 2008

Animal Studies

1. Edwin Landseer, *A dead stag lying on a wheelbarrow* 1845
Coloured chalks on discoloured buff paper
359 x 506 mm.
Signed in chalk with monogram in circle, lower centre: *EL; 1845*
Fitzwilliam Museum PD. 173-1961

2. Edwin Landseer, *Dead stag lying on a bench*
Coloured chalks and some wash on blue paper
359 x 502 mm.
Fitzwilliam Museum PD. 174-1961

Landseer was fascinated by stags throughout his career and feature in many of his most iconic paintings. In these rapidly-drawn sketches he explores the contortions of the bodies of two dead stags.

3. John Frederick Lewis, *A wounded Roebuck*
Black chalk, with watercolour and bodycolour heightened with white on paper, mounted with false margins
283 x 408 mm.
Signed in graphite, lower right: *J. F. Lewis.*; inscribed on *verso* of mount: *J. F. Lewis ARA*
Fitzwilliam Museum PD. 98-1950

Lewis is best known as a painter of Orientalist subject matter but also made a number of impressive animal studies. The use of bodycolour allowed watercolour artists produce works of increased density and power.

4. Robert Hills, *Studies of deer*
Graphite and watercolour on paper
151 x 132 mm.
Dated in graphite, lower right: *Dec 30th 1801*
Fitzwilliam Museum no. 761a (3)

5. Robert Hills, *Studies of deer*
Graphite and watercolour on paper
151 x 132 mm.
Inscribed in graphite, lower right; *Dec 29 1801; Dawney*
Fitzwilliam Museum no. 761a (4)

6. John Frederick Lewis, *A Dead Dog*
Black chalk and watercolour on grey paper
282 x 409 mm.
Fitzwilliam Museum PD. 180-1961

7. James Ward, *Study of Lord Somerville's puppies* c. 1805
Graphite and watercolour on paper
Watermark: J RUSE 1802
240 x 334 mm.
Signed in ink with monogram, lower right: *JWD. RA*; inscribed in graphite with a line of shorthand, lower left, and: *Lord Somerville Pups / Spaniel & Cartouche*
Fitzwilliam Museum no. 3366

8. James Ward, *Study of a Spanish ass* 1822
Graphite and watercolour on Bristol board
195 x 227 mm.
Signed in ink with monogram, lower right: *JWD. RA*; inscribed in graphite, lower right, *. . . /Study of a Spanish ass / Brixton Deverell / June -1822*
Fitzwilliam Museum no. 3394b

9. Edwin Landseer, *A shooting pony*
Black and white chalk, traces of red chalk on discoloured grey paper
359 x 502 mm.
Fitzwilliam Museum PD. 175-1961

10. Robert Hills, *Sheet of studies of horses* 1804
Graphite on paper
277 x 203 mm.
Inscribed in graphite with a line of shorthand, lower right and: *July 4th 1804*
Fitzwilliam Museum no. 1363b

In his drawings of animals Hills often uses a soft, rich black graphite pencil and a jagged line which helps to suggest the texture of the beast's coat.

11. Robert Hills, *Studies of horses*
Graphite on paper
274 x 203 mm.
Fitzwilliam Museum no. 1363c

12. James Ward, *Studies of five pigs, lying down*
Graphite and watercolour on paper
281 x 371 mm.
Signed in ink with initials, lower right: *JWD. RA*
Fitzwilliam Museum no. 3386

13. David Cox, *Studies of sheep*
Red and blue-grey chalk on paper
215 x 308 m.
Signature in graphite, lower right: *D. Cox*
In reverse for engraving
Fitzwilliam Museum no. 1339

14. James Ward, *Study of a Sheep* c. 1802-5
Pen and ink, black and white chalk on brown paper, laid down and fixed
205 x 272 mm.
Signed in ink with initials, lower right: *J. W. RA.*; inscribed in ink on *verso* of mount: *Study from Nature.*
Fitzwilliam Museum PD. 27-1992

This drawing has been fixed by Ward, using an egg-white mixture called glair.

15. Robert Hills, *Studies of rams' horns*
Graphite on paper, three sketches in same mount
110 x 176 mm.
Fitzwilliam Museum no. 1365h

16. Robert Hills, *Studies of heads of sheep*
Graphite on paper
108 x 178 mm.
Fitzwilliam Museum no. 1365i

17. Robert Hills, *Studies of rams' heads*
Graphite on paper
110 x 179 mm.
Fitzwilliam Museum no. 1365j

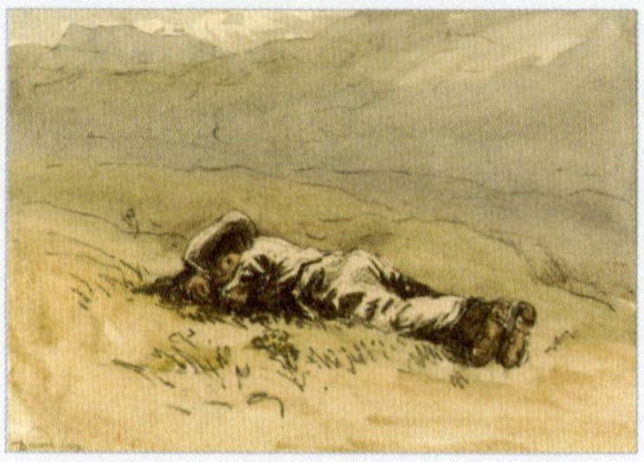

37. David Cox, *Boy lying on his face*

18. Robert Hills, *Sheet of studies of deer*
Graphite on paper
186 x 271 mm.
Fitzwilliam Museum no. 1362b

19. Robert Hills, *Etchings of Cattle comprising Rudiments of Drawings and Groups for the Embellishment of Landscape, the whole executed from Nature by Robert Hills*
London: Publish'd March 21st 1806, by Robert Hills.
125pp. 203 plates, 39 duplicates
Fitzwilliam Museum no. P.4111-R

20. James Ward, *Study of a bull's head*
Graphite and watercolour on paper
125 x 224 mm.
Signature in ink, lower right: *JW. RA*; inscribed on *verso* of mount: *Bull's Eye and Nose*
Fitzwilliam Museum no. 3393a

21. James Ward, *Studies of cows and calves, standing and lying*
Graphite and watercolour on paper
186 x 272 mm.
Signature in graphite: *JW. RA*; inscribed in graphite, lower left: *Tabley; July 20 1811*
Fitzwilliam Museum no. 3384b

22. Robert Hills, *Etchings of Red Deer by Robert Hills*
London: Publish'd Jan 2 1812 by R. Hills
48pp, 62 plates, 1 duplicate
Fallow Deer Drawn from Nature and etch'd by Robert Hills
London, Pub Jan 1st 1813 by R. Hills
53pp, 80 plates
Fitzwilliam Museum no. P.4112-R

23. William Harvey, *Animal studies*
Graphite and Watercolour on Paper
Five studies of various animals, Fitzwilliam Museum no. 779 (14)
Giraffe, no. 779 (22)
Rhinoceros and wild buffalo, no. 779 (28 & 29)
Kangaroo, wombat and other animals, no. 779 (30)

24. Edward Julius Detmold, *The Chimpanzee*
Watercolour on paper
264 x 207 mm.
Signature with monogram, lower left: *EJD*
Fitzwilliam Museum no. 2469

Landscapes and Buildings

25. James Ward, *Study of a piece of rock*
Graphite and watercolour on paper
264 x 370 mm.
Signed in ink with monogram, lower left: *J.Ward. RA*
Fitzwilliam Museum no. 3399b

26. Robert Hills, *Studies of sunset at Windsor Forest*
Graphite and watercolour on paper
223 x 190 mm.
Inscribed in graphite with three lines of shorthand along bottom: *July 28th Windsor Forest*
Fitzwilliam Museum no. 1377

27. Robert Hills, *Landscape with cattle, near Dorking, Surrey*
Watercolour over graphite with traces of gum Arabic on paper
501 x 412 mm.
Signed in watercolour, inner right: *R Hills 1811*; inscribed in graphite on *verso*: *Near Dorking, Surrey*
Fitzwilliam Museum no. 2354

28. William Henry Hunt, *The Outhouse* 1838
Graphite, watercolour and bodycolour on paper
540 x 749 mm.
Fitzwilliam Museum no. 739

William Henry Hunt was trained in the studio of John Varley (1778-1842). The 1820s was a period of transition for Hunt; instead of flat washes, he began to use small strokes of colour, and in the 1830s he added bodycolour in parts. *The Outhouse* demonstrates this change: over preliminary flat washes, Hunt applied loose strokes of colour and gave texture and solidity with scratchy touches of dark pigment applied with a dry brush.

29. Robert Hills, *Study of a lean-to and shed*
Graphite and watercolour on paper
235 x 336 mm.
Inscribed on *verso*: *Hills; 1275*
Fitzwilliam Museum no. 1275

This unfinished sketch of a rural dwelling has been executed on rough paper, on which tiny black and brown specks can be seen.

30. Robert Hills, *Study of barns*
Graphite and watercolour on paper
185 x 330 mm.
Fitzwilliam Museum no. 1369

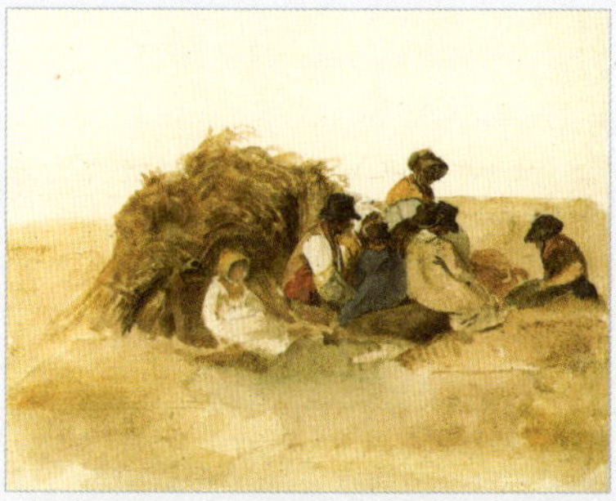

41. Peter De Wint, *Harvesters Resting*

Farmyard Tools

31. Robert Hills, *Studies of ploughs and rakes* 1807
Graphite and watercolour on paper
269 x 204 mm.
Inscribed in graphite with two lines of shorthand, centre right and lower right; inscribed in graphite, lower right: *1807*; inscribed on *verso*: *Hills*
Fitzwilliam Museum no. 1373g

32. Robert Hills, *Study of ploughs*
Graphite and watercolour on paper
265 x 182 mm.
Inscribed in graphite with one line of shorthand, lower left
Fitzwilliam Museum no. 1373e

33. Robert Hills, *Study of a cart*
Graphite and watercolour on paper
109 x 182 mm.
Inscribed in ink with one line of shorthand, lower right; inscribed on *verso* in graphite: *Hills*
Fitzwilliam Museum no. 1373c

Figure Studies

34. William Henry Hunt, *The Gleaner*
Watercolour heightened with white, with surface scratching on paper
283 x 196 mm.
Fitzwilliam Museum no. 1796

Gleaning, or raking up loose stalks, left over from the harvest, was seen as a right of the farm labourer, but the practice declined throughout the nineteenth century. The reality of life as a gleaner is not found, however, in this optimistic portrayal of an immaculately-dressed and rosy-cheeked young girl, holding a plentiful bundle of stalks.

35. Robert Hills, *Studies of a ? milkmaid*
Graphite and watercolour on Whatman paper
Watermark: Whatman 1804
209 x 274 mm.
Fitzwilliam Museum no. 1374c

Despite dairy farms arguably offering the severest labour performed by women, Hills's depiction of a rural worker, like Hunt's *Gleaner*, depicts a worker apparently unaffected by such demanding work.

36. Robert Hills, *Studies of children haymaking*
Graphite and watercolour on paper
302 x 257 mm.
Inscribed in graphite on *verso*: *Hills*
Fitzwilliam Museum no. 1564c

Hills's fascination with clothing is evident here, as he pays close attention to style and texture, and his description of shadow on the back of the young girl's sleeve is exquisitely rendered.

37. David Cox, *Boy lying on his face*
Black chalk and watercolour on paper
176 x 253 mm.
Signature, lower left: *David Cox*
Fitzwilliam Museum no. 1556

This drawing, and no. 39, epitomise Cox's use of a flickering, jerky line, often broken by the roughness of the paper he favoured. Charcoal or black chalk was employed, which was either absorbed by the colour or allowed to show through, depending on which effect was desired.

38. James Ward, *Study of a sleeping boy*
Graphite on paper
189 x 261 mm.
Signed in graphite with monogram, lower centre: *JWard. R.A.*
Fitzwilliam Museum no. 3379b

This sort of single figure study is unusual for Ward. Here he concentrates on the soles of the labourer's boots, while the rest of his body is depicted by a series of loose markings.

39. David Cox, *Study of a seated figure in a landscape*
Charcoal and watercolour on paper, laid down
176 x 253 mm.
Signed in graphite, lower left: *David Cox*
Fitzwilliam Museum no. 1292

During the first half of the nineteenth century both Cox and De Wint demonstrated nostalgia for open fields. Cox admired the political pamphleteer, farmer and journalist, William Cobbett (1763-1835). Cobbett, who lived on a farm in Hampshire from 1805-17, began to call himself a Radical in 1806, mainly because of his indignation at the poor pay and miserable conditions suffered by agricultural labourers. The distressed state of English farming continued to preoccupy him during the 1820s. He remarked of labourers in 1821 that they seemed 'miserably poor ... in my whole life I never saw human wretchedness equal to this'.

40. Robert Hills, *Studies of a gardener, children and wheelbarrows*
Graphite and watercolour on paper
305 x 233 mm.
Fitzwilliam Museum no. 1564a

41. Peter De Wint, *Harvesters Resting*
Watercolour with gum Arabic over graphite on paper
324 x 340 mm.
Fitzwilliam Museum no. 1583

This watercolour, with broad, loose washes of colour, sums up De Wint's painterly approach. The paper has been left blank on the top half, which, along with the low viewpoint, conveys the sense of an endless sky.

The poet John Clare wrote to De Wint in 1829; 'these rough sketches taken in the field that breathes with the living freshness of open air and sunshine where the blending and harmony of earth and sky are in such a happy unison of greens and greys that a flat bit of scenery on a few inches of paper appear as many miles'.

42. Robert Hills, *Studies of children*
Graphite and watercolour on paper
300 x 224 mm.
Fitzwilliam Museum no. 1564d

Bibliography

Albany Gallery, *Robert Hills 1769-1844*, London, 1968

Bayard, Jane, *Works of splendour and imagination: the exhibition watercolour, 1770-1870*, New Haven: Yale Center for British Art, c1981

Bermingham, Ann, *Landscape and ideology: the English rustic tradition, 1740-1860*, London: Thames & Hudson, 1987

Collins, E. J. T., 'Harvest Technology and Labour Supply in Britain, 1790-1870', *The Economic History Review*, New Series, Vol. 22, No. 3 (Dec., 1969), pp. 453-473

Evans, R. J., *The Victorian age, 1815-1914*, London: Edward Arnold, 1968

Fitzwilliam Museum, *Gilpin to Ruskin: Drawing Masters and their Manuals, 1800-1860*, Cambridge & Grasmere, 1988

Fox, H. S. A. & R. A. Butlin, (eds.) *Change in the Countryside: Essays on Rural England, 1500-1900*, London: Institute of British Geographers, 1979

Hardie, Martin, *Water-colour painting in Britain*, London: Batsford, 1966-68, 3 vols.

Horn, Pamela, *Life and Labour in Rural England, 1760-1850*, Basingstoke: Macmillan, 1987

Laing Art Gallery, *John Frederick Lewis, RA 1805-1876*, Newcastle, 1971

Lambourne, Maureen, 'A Watercolourist's Countryside: the art of Robert Hills', *Country Life*, 144 (1986)

Long, Basil, 'Robert Hills', *Walker's Quarterly*, 12 (1923)

Lord, John (ed), *Peter De Wint 1784-1849: for the common observer of life and nature*, Aldershot: Lund Humphries, 2007

Munro, Jane, *James Ward RA, 1769-1859*, Cambridge: Fitzwilliam Museum, c1991

Munro, Jane, *British Landscape Watercolours 1750-1850*, Cambridge: Fitzwilliam Museum, 1994

Payne, Christiana, *Toil and plenty: images of the agricultural landscape in England, 1780-1890*, New Haven; London: Yale University Press, 1993

Pyne, William Henry, *Etchings of Rustic Figures for the Embellishment of Landscape*, London, 1814

Roget, John Lewis, *A history of the 'Old Water-colour Society'*, London: Longmans, Green & Co., 1891

Rosenthal, Michael, *British landscape painting*, Oxford: Phaidon, 1982

Williams, Iolo, 'Robert Hills (1779-1844)', *The Burlington Magazine for Connoisseurs*, Vol. 86, No. 503, Feb. 1945

Notes

1. Martin Hardie, *Water-colour painting in Britain*, II: 140
2. John Lewis Roget, *A history of the 'Old Water-colour Society'*, I: 175
3. Roget, I: 130, quoting Robert Hills
4. Jane Bayard, *Works of Splendour and Imagination*, 6
5. Bayard, 7
6. Jane Munro, *British Landscape Watercolours*, 17
7. Basil Long, 'Robert Hills', *Walker's Quarterly*, No. 23, 1929, 18
8. Bayard, 15
9. *Gilpin to Ruskin: Drawing Masters and their Manuals, 1800-1860*, 11
10. Munro, 17
11. Ann Bermingham, *Landscape and ideology: the English rustic tradition, 1740-1860*, 1
12. R. J. Evans, *The Victorian age 1815-1914*, 1
13. Bermingham, 73
14. Bermingham, 76
15. Bermingham, 77
16. John Lord (ed), *Peter De Wint 1784-1849: for the common observer of life and nature*, 32
17. Lord, 40
18. Christiana Payne, *Toil and plenty: images of the agricultural landscape in England, 1780-1890*, 46
19. Quoted in Long, 25
20. Hardie, II: 141
21. Bayard, 19
22. Michael Rosenthal, *British Landscape Painting*, 96
23. William Henry Pyne, *Etchings of Rustic Figures for the Embellishment of Landscape*, 5
24. Quoted in Evans, 3
25. Pyne, 5
26. E. J. T. Collins, 'Harvest Technology and labour Supply in Britain, 1790-1870', *The Economic History Review*, New Series, Vol. 22, No. 3 (Dec., 1969), pp. 453-473
27. John R. Walton, 'Mechanization in Agriculture: A Study in the Adoption Process', in *Change in the Countryside: Essays on Rural England, 1500-1900*, eds. H. S. A. Fox & R. A. Butlin, 24
28. Pyne, 5-6
29. Jane Munro, *James Ward RA, 1769-1859*, 8
30. Maureen Lambourne, 'A Watercolourist's Countryside: the art of Robert Hills', *Country Life*, 144 (1986)
31. For example, George Monbiot, 'Credit crunch? The real crisis is global hunger', *Guardian*, April 15th 2008; Aditya Chakrabortty, 'Fields of gold', *Guardian*, April 16th 2008

Nicola Gauld, Research Associate, The Fitzwilliam Museum

I would like to thank Jane Munro, Senior Assistant Keeper of Paintings, Drawing & Prints, for granting me this opportunity, Lowell Libson, for kindly supporting the exhibition, Andrew Morris, Head of Photographic Dept, for producing the images, and Bryan Clarke, Senior Paper Conservator, for his work on the watercolours.